MW01241347

Copyright 2023 by LeeGacy Elevation, LLC

Printed in the United States of America. First Printing, 2023

ISBN: 979-8-9880194-5-9

Author

IG | FB | Twitter: @bball101epd
www.bball101.com

Publisher

IG | FB | Twitter: @wcwriting1
Visit Our Website
Williamscommerce1.com
Williams Commerce, LLC

Table of Contents

Introduction 1

Key 1 5

Key 2 12

Key 3 23

Key 4 31

Key 5 36

Key 6 42

Key 7 47

Key 8 55

Conclusion 72

Introduction

I need to ask a favor of you. I need you not to be offended by the title. I will explain it shortly. What you are about to read could actually change your life as a parent—not just as the parent of an athlete, but as an everyday parent.

I get excited about many things. But I can honestly say that this may be the most excited I've ever been about anything I've done in the game of basketball. My company has helped hundreds of athletes earn Division I, Division II, Division III, NAIA, and Junior College (JUCO) scholarships. We have been fortunate to have an impact in ways that many will never fully grasp. The 70+ first-generation college graduates who have come through our program represent perhaps our greatest accomplishment.

The countless lawyers, doctors, entrepreneurs, and even future Anderson Coopers (CNN's Omar Jimenez) and Oprah Winfreys (Aleah Hordges) all get me excited! Their successes evoke immense pride and satisfaction. But not like the writing of this book. This book represents thousands of conversations that have taken place throughout the years. Thousands of hours of helping parents navigate through the "land mine"– rich field of youth sports.

I am so thankful that I am able to share my experiences with you. My perspective comes from a deep and rich history of developing athletes, many of whom started at extremely young ages. Because of this, I have been able to see full athletic career life cycles. But what is even more of a blessing is having six children of my own with personalities that span the gamut.

I have made many mistakes, and I continue to make them. However, three decades of being a parent has taught me what a classroom never could: that "parenting" isn't always about what we do. It is often about what we don't do. Sometimes phenomenal parenting is allowing our offspring to figure it out on their own. But here is the kicker: this book is not written from some perch. It is written from the trenches. I, too, could be the reason my kids don't reach their full potential. I am not immune from falling prey to the very issues we are about to discuss. Only

2

time will tell if this book will age well with my own children who are young basketball players.

I started developing athletes in the early 2000s. I have seen a lot in this game of basketball. I have watched many parents encourage their children and push them to some amazing accomplishments. I have also seen parents do the opposite. This book is about those observations. It is also about figuring out how to guide your young athlete with confidence.

Yes, I understand better than most that every child is different. However, every child is human. There are basic human needs that have to be met, regardless of someone's personality, ethnicity, and/or religion. In Maslow's 5 Levels of Human Needs, "Self-Esteem" lies at level 4. On Maslow's chart, "Self-Esteem" encompasses confidence, achievement, the respect of others, and the need to be a unique individual. My goal is to show that this is accomplished through both positive experiences and perceived negative events.

"Perceived" means exactly that. What looks like a deterrent or detriment can actually be a seed of success. It is my goal, as an author, to get you to understand that all that happens to your child could actually be happening for your child. I will elaborate later. This is as much a spiritual journey as it is a physical one. It is time for you, as a parent or steward over your child's life, to understand that. This is about skillfully allowing life to teach its own lessons, along with whatever you are teaching your child.

It is my hope that this book of dos and don'ts will help you help your child navigate this journey and achieve great success. It is also my hope that if basketball isn't a deep passion for your child, you can use this book to help identify your child's passion. Or, at the very least, attach basketball to a passion (i.e., education) for long enough to receive all the tremendous benefits that this beautiful sport has to offer. Regardless of what you might think, either of these outcomes is an enormous victory. ENJOY!

Dorian A. Lee, Author

Key 1

DO: UNDERSTAND PARENTING STYLES

You and I are about to have the talk. The talk that I have had with nearly every parent since I started the journey of developing young athletes. I would like to start by saying that we're going to have some fun with this book. As I stated in the Introduction, I want to make sure that you don't take offense to the title. It is designed to get your attention by using a term that basketball players have used for eons. Players use the word "trash" to describe themselves and others when they don't play well. "Trash" is the term we use in the game of basketball to describe poor performance. When someone doesn't play well, we say that they "played like trash." If a player doesn't play well, they tend to say themselves that "I played like trash." If our team doesn't play well, we say that "we all played like trash."

But I will keep it real. Offensive or not, there is some truth to the statement. Our parenting styles can have a lasting impact on our kids' personalities. So much so that it is important to learn about these styles.

The same parenting style can look vastly different for each child. Yes, you can have a specific parenting style, but based on the child's personality, it might look different to them. If you didn't know by now, there are four parenting styles: authoritarian, authoritative, permissive, and uninvolved. Once you have a deeper understanding of each style, you'll understand which one will best help your children to succeed both academically and athletically. Now, understand, there will be times when you'll venture into all of these parenting styles. However, I want to focus on the parenting style that you predominantly use.

The authoritarian parent is the "no holds barred" parent. In this parenting style, there is very little latitude for children to break the rules set by their parents. The punishments can be severe, but that does not mean abusive. However, authoritarian parents have an extremely strict parenting style. They place high expectations on children with little responsiveness. As an authoritarian parent, you focus more on obedience, discipline, and control than on nurturing an ascending democratic environment for your child.

One of the most profound examples of this style of parenting is that of my good friend, Chuck Nwagwu. Chuck and I forged a friendship as I trained his daughter Morgan Robinson-Nwagwu, a Division I athlete, for years. Chuck is a former walk-on at Jackson State University (JSU) who, with his blue-collar work ethic, ridiculously competitive spirit, and tremendous strength, became a starter for the Tigers—an incredibly daunting task that speaks to his dedication.

Chuck's work ethic forged the way on the basketball court. Chuck was also a really good student. However, his father, Dr. 'Emeka Nwagwu, was an associate professor at JSU at the time and felt Chuck's academic performance—he held a 3.2 GPA—was subpar. His father made the decision that he would have to quit the team. Dr. Nwagwu was an incredible father who raised an incredible young man. But as it pertained to academics, he was nonnegotiable. Chuck really had no say in the matter.

My father, Frank E. Lee, Sr., as well as my mother, Doris A. Lee, also had many authoritarian areas in their parenting style. As it pertained to respect, manners, or wasting of food, money, or time, my father was not to be played with. My mother, who was an esteemed educator, was extremely critical when it came to things like handwriting, quality of work, cleanliness, and grammar—both verbal and written. I remember being slapped once for not including my middle initial in my signature. It is hilarious to me now. But it wasn't at the time. I am certain Chuck and I would agree that we could have benefited from more authoritative parenting in these particular areas.

The authoritative parent puts effort into creating and maintaining a positive relationship with their child. They tend to explain the reasons behind their rules. These parents enforce rules and give consequences but take the child's feelings into consideration.

The permissive parent sets rules but rarely enforces them. The permissive parent doesn't give out consequences very often. They think their child will learn best with little interference. They believe that "children will be children" and that "they are just children!"

The uninvolved parent means just that. They are extremely detached from their kids apart from providing the basic necessities. They also don't spend a lot of emotionally focused time with their children. Uninvolved parents rarely ask their kids about their day at school, homework, or grades. This doesn't mean they're bad parents. My father was a phenomenal man, but he was uninvolved in my athletic life. He didn't take me to practices and didn't come to games. My dad wasn't an athlete. He taught me many valuable lessons outside of the sport. But growing up, he was virtually nonexistent in my sporting life.

Once you have reviewed these parenting styles, make an honest assessment of what style your parenting primarily falls under. Once you've identified your parenting style, it's time to get to work—meaning that we need to continue to hone more authoritative traits.

There are times when all parenting styles can and should be used strategically. For instance, there might be times when your child doesn't respect your time or your efforts to give them the resources they need to reach their goals—or at least the goals they have expressed they want to reach. It is okay, at that point, to become "uninvolved" for periods of time to show that your investment of resources and time should be respected. However, maintaining an authoritative style will give the greatest long-term benefit to your child.

REFLECT

Take a moment to evaluate how you parent, not just as a parent of an athlete, but in a variety of ways. Are there areas where your style of parenting differs? Is your parenting style consistent in all areas? Are you simply parenting the way that you were parented? Or have you developed your own style?

ACT

1. Focus on become more aware of your parenting. Pay particularly close attention to how you respond to your child. If you are, perhaps, irritated by interruptions, begin to ask yourself "why" that bothers you. You will find that your reaction is often conditioned triggers that you honestly don't give much thought to prior to responding. See if you can start to intercept those responses and evaluate if they are effective. Also note that with each child, the response could be vastly different.

Key 2

DO: ACCURATELY ASSESS YOUR CHILD'S ... UMMM ...EVERYTHING!

If I had a dollar for every time I heard a parent say that "my child loves basketball," I would be one of the wealthiest men in the world. But I am not. Only one thing could make me even wealthier: if I were given a dollar for every time a parent refused to believe me when I told them that their child didn't love the game of basketball. Delusion is real among doting parents.

Throughout the years, I have often been the first to tell parents that their child didn't want to play basketball. How did I know? Was I clairvoyant? Was I spiritually enlightened? No, I knew because the kid told me! Like literally told me. These have been, most often, very difficult conversations. I've encouraged several multi-sport athletes to focus on other sports. I've also been accused of not believing in a child for doing so. On the contrary, I believed in the child's talent in other sports so much that I actually encouraged them to leave the sport I love.

Knowing what is required of this sport and knowing that the child could not meet those requirements forced me to have an open and honest dialogue with the athlete and their parent. This dialogue was, and will always be, based on my understanding of what is required of this sport and my experience helping young athletes meet those requirements for coaches at every level.

It is to be noted that every kid that I encouraged to pursue a sport for which they were better suited became a scholarship recipient in that sport. One, Gerald Rashard Everett, even played in the Super Bowl LIII recently. Gerald, like many kids, loved basketball but was somewhat of a tweener. But he had an incredibly athletic body. He attended a guard camp that I held along with Jay Hernandez, Charlotte Hornet's assistant. Jay and I both thought that with his height and skillset, it would be a difficult path to high-major basketball. So after assessing this young man's gifts, I asked a simple question: "Does he play football?" His parents said, "No." I said that he should. "I think he would be an amazing wide receiver or tight end. He is considered a big receiver. He will get a scholarship."

I never thought about that day again until I received a phone call from the friend who had referred him to the camp. He told me that he wanted to thank me because, after that day, Gerald focused strictly on football. He played football for the first time the following season, his senior season, at Columbia High School in Decatur, Georgia. On March 22, 2022, Gerald signed a two-year $12 million contract with the Los Angeles Chargers.

I get really emotional when I think about it. What if I had kept my mouth shut or told them what they wanted to hear versus what was in my heart? Had I not gotten the call, I would never have known that my words changed the course of this outstanding young man's life. Many other parents have also returned to thank me for my advice, even though it was contentious (to say the least) at first discussion.

Samantha was a parent whose son was a good high school player but not necessarily a high-level NCAA Division I athlete. This isn't always a physical assessment. Oftentimes, this is based on intangible attributes that may or may not be present in the athlete, such as work ethic, maturity, ability to process information quickly, and awareness. I shared with her that I thought that, with work, he would be perfectly suited for Division II basketball and potentially have an outstanding career. She accused me of being "jealous" of her son and not wanting him to "exceed the level" at which I played. I had to remind her that the survival of my business revolved around players exceeding any and all of my accomplishments! He quit basketball two years later. Having had time to reflect, she apologized. She realized just how poorly she had assessed her son's ability, drive, mental toughness, and love for the game.

I really can't make this stuff up! See, there's a reason I often cringe when I hear a parent say that their child loves basketball. I cringe because I know what love looks like and how closely it resembles obsession! Of the thousands of players that I have been privileged to develop throughout the years, at every level, only a handful possessed that obsessive love that is needed to elevate them above all obstacles, setbacks, challenges, or any other synonym that describes the necessary adversity that one has to face in order to grow into the player they desire to be.

However—this will shock you and may sound contradictory—you don't have to love basketball to be successful at it. You simply have to attach basketball to something you love! For example, many athletes have been motivated by getting their parents out of poverty. Others simply want to surpass their parents' athletic careers. Some want to achieve academic success at some of the greatest institutions in the country without having to pay for it. There are countless reasons that athletes have excelled at the game of basketball outside of loving the actual game. But what they did have was a big enough reason why and a healthy respect for the game and what it could provide. Remember that respect and love are very closely related virtues.

I must add that there's a difference between love and deep liking. Love adds another dimension to the connection you have with the game of basketball: commitment. See, commitment is the ability to do what you said you would long after the emotion in which you said it has passed. When you like something, the strength of your commitment is low. When you love something, the strength of your commitment is extremely high.

As a parent, just think about relationships—marriage in particular. It is much harder to walk away from a marriage, because of the investment of time, love, emotions, finances, dreams, etc., than it is to walk away from someone you have dated for a month. When you love something, you put up with and fight through many obstacles because you deem it worthy. Even after romantic love has faded, the commitment often still lingers. That is what separates loving from liking. So, ultimately, when I hear of people quitting the sport of basketball because of a coach, politics, injuries, or any obstacle, I automatically assume that the love or the why did not outweigh the perceived adversity.

But the delusional assessment of one's child does not stop at assuming they love the sport. Parents often poorly assess their athlete's current ability, work ethic, potential, emotional intellect, and desire. There is science behind the notion that perception is projection. As parents, we often unload our aspirations, beliefs, emotions, and fears onto our children. In many respects, there is nothing wrong with that. But we can only project to the level of our own awareness, experience, and maturity.

What do I mean by that? What I mean is this: if you have no understanding of the landscape of youth sports, then you are more than likely using information that comes from different fields and attempting to adopt it in the world of sports. It also comes from the "stands." If not the stands, then we follow any advice that comes from social media as long as the person has a "blue check" and 100K followers. Everyone who owns a microphone and a cell phone and has a social media page on any platform is now an expert. If this isn't the case, then where are you getting your information from? This is by far one of the most important questions that you could ever ask yourself.

My primary concern with getting information via other parents who are facing the same issues is that we often attempt to replicate techniques that were designed for one person. There are some spiritual aspects to all successful journeys. In other words, there are consistent themes, such as desire, work ethic, commitment to developing ability, and resilience. Also, we're often asking people who are on the journey with us. So there is no true outcome data. They are simply winging it. Just like you.

In my somewhat experienced opinion, one must focus on seeking expert counsel. This should consist of a wide array of people, including the parents of athletes who have reached the levels that you desire your child to achieve and professionals such as team coaches, player development coaches, and recruiting service experts. The importance of this part of the process cannot be understated. But it is the part of the process that is most often neglected.

Also, people often reject those who don't paint a narrative quite like the one they want. Basically, many parents refuse to listen to those who don't tell them what they want to hear. The expert is ignored in favor of a more "appealing" narrative. Like I mentioned, people are looking for those who tell them what they want to hear, not what they need to hear.

REFLECT

Assess your child's love and commitment to the sport by asking these questions:

1. Does your child truly eat, sleep, and breathe basketball?
2. If the answer is yes, then does your child eat, sleep, and breathe as a spectator or as a participant? In other words, do they love the culture or do they love the sport?
3. Does your child need excessive prodding to practice or work on their games?
4. Does your child constantly display attitude when asked to give more effort?
5. Have you ever stated that your child is lazy?
6. Have you ever stated that you want it more than your child does?
7. Have you sought guidance from those with legitimate experience of the path you are traveling? Do they have any motivation to tell you anything other than the truth?

ACT

1. Set up a meeting with a reputable player development coach, college recruiter, or college coach, and get an understanding of what high school and college coaches are looking for in athletes at every position—the types of personalities and character traits. Not just on the court but off the court as well. This will give you a much better understanding of what is expected.

2. Set up an evaluation with a player development coach or anyone who can assess your young athlete's skill level. Be mindful of trainers who are looking to simply fill their roster. What do I mean by that? Those who just want to get paid. One simple and effective way to get honest feedback is to tell the player development coach that you live out of town. Tell them that you've heard they were incredible at assessing talent and want to get strong feedback on where your child is, relative to grade and age, in the development process.

3. Have a conversation with your child after completing the questions that were listed under REFLECT. Let your child know that your love for

them is not contingent on whether or not they play a sport, and tell them you understand that many kids like the attention they get from doing things that their parents want them to do. Let them know that there is zero pressure to do it for you, the parent. However, reinforce that if they are going to do it, there must be effort on both sides. In addition, tell them that everything should be done with a high level of excellence. Let them understand that you will support them to the extent to which they commit. That isn't about just showing up to team practices and games. It involves spending intimate time honing their craft.

Key 3

DON'T: SHIELD YOUR CHILD FROM ALL "NEGATIVE" EXPERIENCES

Folks, I get it! We don't want to see our children in pain. And we want them to avoid pain at all costs. That is why this thing called "life" is designed the way it is. Kids don't pop out as independent individuals. According to New York Times bestselling author Dr. Stephen Covey, children should go through the stages of dependency, then independence, then, ultimately and optimally, interdependency. That is why we were chosen. But we were chosen to be stewards, not owners. We are to serve as guides. I have a simple question: Do you want your kids to be great at something? If the answer is yes, then it is of the highest importance that you understand that part of the process of becoming successful is failing. You do not become successful in spite of failures. You become successful because of failures! By learning from failure, making adjustments, and redirecting one's course, one develops resilience. Redirected failure is success!

Now, granted, this book is by no means a religious text. But I can't help but think of the first part of Romans 8:28 where it states that "All things work together for good ..." In other words, as mentioned before, we have to stop believing that things happen to us and start to believe that things happen for us! For us to elevate, for us to dig deep, for us to see things in ourselves that would not have been revealed had it not been for the "adversity." These are often the very things that will shape your young athlete into exactly what you want them to become.

There is no such thing as succeeding your way to success or winning your way to winning. I find it difficult to understand how parents, when reflecting on their own lives, miss the fact that they learned many valuable lessons from their failures. And if they look at it honestly, how "bad" did they really turn out? I believe that there should be small adjustments made to parenting styles, but I don't believe that parenting should be overhauled and dramatically altered from one generation to the next—just a slight improvement that yields better results for each generation. The reason I'm talking about parenting is because parenting, on and off the court, is very similar, if not the same.

In my very good friend Dr. Mary Stone's book *Fortitude*, she speaks of many of these life lessons. I have often said that basketball is life sped up throughout 32, 40, 44, or 48 minutes, depending on what level you play. Literally everything you need to do to be successful in life you also need to do to be successful on the basketball court. You will lead at times. You will also follow. You will be asked to cooperate. You have to become resilient. You have to develop physical and mental toughness. You have to strategize and execute. You will have to follow directives. You will be dependent, independent, and, most importantly, interdependent all at the same time. How do you play when you're ahead on the court and in life? How do you play when you're behind on the court and in life? These are lessons that undoubtedly prepare you for life.

Parents spend too much time plotting the course for their child. Within that plotting is a plan to avoid any adversity and any obstacles along the way. In other words, parents are attempting to prepare the road for the child and not the child for the road. These adversities will shape your child into the player and, more importantly, the person that the parent wants them to become. The earlier that players have to deal with adversity, the better.

Take, for example, the peculiar case of Mike Tyson, boxing legend and at one time the most feared man on the planet. Mike Tyson was invincible—or so we thought. He went so long without losing that when he finally lost, after thirty professional fights, he could not recover. I believe that if he had lost earlier in his career, he would have reigned much longer as heavyweight champion of the world. The once beautifully skilled fighter became an angry fighter, obsessed with winning by intimidation long after those who once feared him no longer did. He missed an incredible opportunity to adjust and get back to the elite preparation and skill that he once had. Tyson could have regained his position atop the world of boxing. Yet not having encountered adversity early on, as well as poor counsel, was eventually his undoing as a boxer.

Believing in your child, trusting your child, and supporting your child has everything to do with knowing your child. Sometimes we have to extend "tough love." Tough love doesn't mean abusive love. Tough love is understanding when to push and pull and when to do nothing. We as parents are often convinced that it's what we give to our kids that makes the difference. However, many times we give by taking away. For instance, if a child doesn't respect all you do for them, there's absolutely nothing wrong with scaling back—having them sit out of a year of sports or, if they're continuously late getting ready for practice, no longer taking them. Or take them but don't let them participate. There are a bunch of different ways to add to their lives by subtracting things from it.

REFLECT

Ask yourself, as a parent, these questions:

1. What is the most important gift that I can give my child?
2. Do I understand stewardship?
3. What is the worst that could happen if I let my child fall flat on their face?

Once these questions are answered, post them where they can be viewed quickly and often.

ACT

1. Think back to a time when you protected your child from a negative experience. Now visualize yourself acting differently and allowing your child to go through the experience. But visualize it working out anyway!

2. Create your Creed of Parenting. Here is an example: I am a parent. I believe that life teaches many valuable lessons. My children are not me. They have their own life and journey. I am a steward over the lives of my children. I believe that they have in them all they will ever need to be successful. I am responsible for providing opportunities that match my child(ren)'s effort. I will not internalize my children's successes or failures. I understand that I am here to guide and not to control. I will allow those placed in my child(ren)'s life to play the role that they were meant to play without interference on my part. I will fight for my child only when it is completely and utterly necessary or where they cannot fight for themselves. I will be honest with myself and my child concerning whether the effort, focus, and

work ethic matches what my child says that they want. If not, it is my responsibility to help them find what it is that gives them the passion, desire, and commitment to stick with it. I will not, under any circumstances, enable my child. I will deliver my child as a prepared, confident, and useful citizen to the world.

Key 4

DO: Allow Your Child to Fight Certain Battles

Hear ye, hear ye! Better yet, listen! Parents, as part of their overall need to keep pain and adversity away from their children, often find themselves fighting fights that were meant for their children to fight. I am all for supporting, defending, and generally protecting your child. But do not become an enabler. I have had far too many conversations with young athletes where every time I asked them a pivotal question, one that could get to the root of what needed to be acknowledged, the parent interjected to give me the "answer" that the child was "about" to give. Now, we all know that it isn't the real answer. But you get my point.

What you will start to find, as you read each chapter of this book, is how each chapter is different, yet they are all interrelated. This book is about building and not controlling your athlete. It is about flow.

I have recognized throughout the years that many of the toughest parents had the softest kids. The loudest parents had the quietest kids. The parents who thought everything their children did was adorable had the most obnoxious kids. The parents who had the most money and gave their children everything seemed to have the children who didn't always see the value of what was being provided.

What I'm saying is this: we don't necessarily want our kids to do what we do or do the opposite of what we do. We want them to develop their own skill at handling many diverse and adverse situations. So in every situation, even if a parent steps in, the player must have some role in expressing how they feel and addressing any concerns head-on.

Effective interpersonal communication is an art— a dying one at that. This skill will come in handy regardless of what career or field your young athlete chooses to pursue. It will strengthen relationships, partnerships, and friendships.

David had a world of talent. But early on I realized that because he came from an affluent background, his goals always had ultimatums. He would say, "I want to play college ball. But only if it is Division I." He would also say that "I'm not interested in playing professional basketball if it's not the NBA!" If he didn't like a school or a coach, his mom would talk to the coach or he would change schools. He just couldn't communicate effectively. But because his mom always had his back financially, he lacked the hunger needed to get through the obstacles. He would eventually quit—having never really fought any of his own battles.

With the advent of social media and improvements in telecommunications, many people have moved further and further away from face-to-face interaction and communication, thus removing all the biofeedback that is necessary for effective dialogue and conversation. What do I mean by biofeedback? This means the body language, tone, and words that make it possible to truly ascertain what is going on.

So many of our young athletes and, quite frankly, many parents lack the necessary skills to handle situations face-to-face. There is far more passive-aggressive and circumvented communication than there once was. How to Win Friends and Influence People, by Dale Carnegie, is one of the greatest books that a parent could ever hand their child. It will help them develop the ability to tactfully and tactilely handle delicate conversations—in other words, to have a way with words. This will give your kids a fighting chance when they are fighting for themselves.

REFLECT

Ask yourself, as a parent, these questions:

1. In your absence, can your child have respectful conversations with coaches and/or teachers concerning things like playing time or making up missed assignments?

2. What is the worst that could happen if you let your child fight their own battles?

ACT

1. Purchase How to Win Friends and Influence People by Dale Carnegie.
2. Read it!
3. Have your child read it.
4. Quiz them on the book.

Key 5

DO: Fully Understand the Politics of The Game

I want to share with you my opinion on a topic that we've all discussed on numerous occasions. I remember my dad saying this word when I was growing up, and I didn't understand what it meant. He always used the term politics. I just remember hearing the word. But as I got older it began to make more sense to me.

Many people who don't know what I do believe that I spend the majority of my day running athletes around cones and chairs. But the bulk of my day is spent speaking to parents, coaches, agents, and, most importantly, players concerning the issues they're facing amongst each other—whether it be players having issues with parents or vice versa, players having issues with their coaches or vice versa, agents having issues with their players, and so on and so on.

I have repeated over and over some simple things to help everyone get on the same page. But there is one question that I always ask: Is politics only an issue when it is not in your favor? What I mean is that, in this world of sports, we are either going to be the beneficiaries or the victims of politics. I find that whenever I discuss politics, it is rooted in victimization, or rather someone isn't getting what they want.

My next question is: "Well, when you have gotten playing time, even when you were playing terribly, did you lobby for the person who was playing behind you to get a chance?" or "When you got tickets to the Beyoncé concert because your dad knew the stage manager, did you give the tickets back so that those who camped outside in tents overnight could get in?" The answer is always the same. So my point is simple. There are two sides to politics, and you will be on one or the other. The key is to become politics-proof!

Being politics-proof revolves around making sure that you remove all nonpolitical barriers: skill, conditioning, IQ, effort, attitude, and energy. All of these can be controlled by you. But how do you know when politics is the game being played? It isn't really hard to tell. Have you completely separated yourself from the other players at your position? This question is by far the most important one. Players often use arbitrary barometers to measure themselves against others. I have heard players say, "I am a better shooter than so-and-so!" Really?

How has that been assessed? Has it been proven by some established metric? Individual team shooting drills? A higher percentage in scrimmages? I have also heard, "I have more skill!" But do you play harder, smarter, and more disciplined? Do you see where this is headed? It's always important to know how your child is being assessed so that they can focus on winning those assessments.

Sport is a meritocracy when there is a skill-based separation between players. Politics comes into play when there is no definable separation. Then a coach can choose based on a multitude of variables: seniority, fondness, commitment to other players, and promises made to other players and parents. Once you have a true assessment of where your child is in terms of (1) separation from others in their position, and (2) skillset in comparison to others in their position, you can make a business-related decision to transfer them to a place where there is a need for what that athlete brings to the table. They should spend 90 percent of their time getting better and showing it at every opportunity. You know when your child is truly better than another player. Awareness is king. Be honest with yourself so that you can take the necessary steps to rectify the situation if your child is indeed the victim of politics.

That being said, I have to acknowledge that there is also a capitalist undercurrent to athletics at almost every level. It is often the determining factor in decisions. It has become even more apparent with the increasing popularity of players on social media. Coaches now understand the immense attention that can be brought to programs by players who already have a strong following. Oftentimes, there are players on other teams who are better. But the difference in standard isn't big enough for the coach to pass up the three million marketing impressions that come along with that player. Player rankings also come into play when talent level among players is equal.

We see this played out at the highest levels. Pro coaches are often fired because they refuse to give playing time to the players that coaches don't feel they can win with. However, the organization feels that those players should play because of the heftiness of their contracts. Why? Because money talks. The sooner you realize this, the sooner you can position your child as an authentic marketing piece and navigate the art of "playing the game!"

ONLY REFLECT

1. Think back to a time when you were a beneficiary of politics. How did you respond?

2. Think back to a time when you were a victim of politics. How did you respond?

Key 6

DON'T: Make Excuses –
"My Baby Can Do No Wrong" Syndrome

I saved the greatest killer of them all for my last DON'T—the epitome of enabling. This is very similar to fighting all your child's battles. Everything but your child is the problem. It is the coach's fault. It is the school's fault. It is the team's fault. It is the teacher's fault. The coaches were picking on your child. It was the play calling. It was the fact that your child didn't eat. It was the fact that they just ate. It was the fact that the gym hasn't been open for your child to get shots up. It was the bracket that they put their team in. And, of course, the referees were horrible. There are so many more excuses, but I will stop there.

My junior college coach, the late Oscar James, often barked, "Excuses are the crutch of the weak!" The only problem was, I was a tad bit slow. Because of his choice of preposition, I thought he meant "crutch of the week" like "plays of the week"! Yeah, I was that slow. Once I replaced "of" with "for," I got it: "Excuses are crutches for the weak!" Man, that makes so much sense. And even worse, when those excuses are made by a parent, it makes their child even weaker.

Being a parent is one of the hardest jobs that we will ever have. However, it is also by far one of the most rewarding. I know it is difficult for us to see our kids as the world often sees them. We have a tendency to see what we want to see and discard what we find in our kids that isn't pleasant. That is the result of evolutionary design so that we don't abandon our kids. But I am here to tell you that your kids can be lazy. Who knew? And your kids can be manipulative. I often hear parents say that they don't believe their kid did what someone else said they did, even when the child exhibits the same behavior in front of the parent. Absolute denial.

Believing in your child, trusting your child, and supporting your child has everything to do with knowing your child. Children for whom others have made excuses grow up to be adults who make excuses. Make a decision—because that is what it is, a decision—never to let your child off the hook for poor decisions and less-than-positive behavior. That doesn't mean you can't empathize. Just make sure you don't condone. Love can be blind when it comes to our children.

I do want to talk about one excuse in particular that has become the excuse of all excuses. That excuse is "That's just their personality!" I need you to understand, right now, that the game of basketball or any other sport, job, or organization doesn't care about your child's personality—only about their ability to perform the task at hand. And part of the job requirement for being a basketball player—drumroll please—is the ability to communicate! The "that's just my child's personality" excuse is also used when they don't pick up instructions quickly enough. It is used when they don't talk with their teammates. It is their excuse for not playing hard.

As mentioned before, communication skills have fallen off tremendously because of the over-utilization of nonverbal communication platforms. This includes social media, emails, and texts. I have found that, since I started in the early 2000s, athletes' verbal communication skills have gotten worse.

Compare basketball with a job posting that has a list of requirements. The listed requirements are nonnegotiable. If the job requires presentations in front of others, face-to-face interactions, and making sales calls, then it has no regard for your personality. Your personality has to conform to the job description and not vice versa. Basketball is no different. You are required to communicate with coaches, teammates, and referees. You are required to listen, execute, follow, lead, and defer at different times. So to make excuses that your child is not getting a fair shake because the coach wants them to do something outside of their personality is absurd. I've seen the quietest of kids joke, play, and roast when among friends, yet they are considered "quiet" kids. Think about that for a second. Everyone gets excited about something: food, tickets, a dunk, a touchdown, a roller-coaster ride or a home run. So the ability is there. That is why there should be no excuses made for not adhering to the "job requirements"!

REFLECT

Take the time to reflect on times when you made excuses for your child. This is a very difficult assignment because you probably don't believe that you were making excuses for them. Maybe it was with a teacher or coach or neighbor. I don't know what experiences you can draw from, but it's important to do it.

ACT

Once you've recalled those times, reevaluate the role that your child played in it all and your own role. Did you handle it in the right way? Is there anything you could have done or said differently? Discernment is the greatest skill we can have when dealing with our young athletes. Develop the skill of discernment by shifting your perspective to that of the child, the parent, and the coach. Perspective is perception. Perception is projection.

Key 7

DO: Make sure your child can actually "BALL!"

Everything we have covered up to this moment is absolutely irrelevant if your child's game is "trash." Meaning that your child simply isn't good at playing basketball. It is incumbent upon you to make sure that your child has the resources to take their game to the next level—and, more importantly, to understand what it will take to chase their goals with a chance that they won't make it.

But regardless of the outcome, the work has to be done. There is no way around it. There is no way to politic your way to being a monster on the court. You will have to develop skill and the understanding of when to deploy that skill. The what, how, when, where, and why is, once again, the key to success in all sporting endeavors.

We are in an era of highly skilled athletes who can do things that we only dreamed of. But, honestly, there are only a few who can actually play the game. Many use their immense skillset at the wrong time and in the wrong scenario. Very little training is designed to make the player's mind reactive and flexible to external stimuli. This is where we have had tremendous success. But there are a ton of well-spirited coaches, trainers, and player development experts who desire to improve players, yet unfortunately haven't found a way to connect the work that is done inside of their program with in-game performance. They simply can't prove that—or don't know whether—what they do translates to games.

Your goal, as a parent, is to make sure that everything you are doing to get your young player better is actually getting them better. Ultimately, although there can be a multitude of measuring sticks, in-game performance is the barometer for improvement. So, questions must be asked when selecting the trifecta of development coaches: player development coach, strength and conditioning coach, and mental toughness coach. I am blessed to be credentialed and experienced in all three areas (BS Health Science, Biomechanics, Speed and Agility, and Mental Toughness). That does not mean I should work with my players in each of these areas, but having a background in each helps me advise parents on what to look for in each coach. There are five questions you should ask of each of your coaches: What is your, background, vision, philosophy, methodology, and short/long-term results.?

BACKGROUND

Past performance can often be used as an indicator of future results. But not always. Experience is important. But what if the experience isn't current? It is important to know what knowledge and expertise a coach has in their wheelhouse. Even with high-end credentials, many coaches get stuck doing the same thing as if it is the infallible word of training. Science, as well as knowledge, is forever evolving. The mere fact that when Babe Ruth played baseball, they were still treating sprained ankles with heat and not ice, is proof of how "expertise" evolves. Listen for words like innovative, transformative, game-changing, etc. It could give you some indication of how forward-thinking a coach can be even with a lengthy and storied career.

VISION

What is the coach's vision for athletes in general and for the athletes who work with this coach specifically? It is good to know where they see the direction of the profession going. You need to know, as well, if that coach has a history of being ahead of the curve. Now, as it pertains to the coach's own roster of athletes, it is good to know where they see their players in comparison to other players who work with other coaches. For example, a coach could say, "I see our kids as those who absolutely maximize their potential, get hurt less often, and are available more often to play!" That tells you what kind of thing to expect for your child if they are to work with that specific coach.

PHILOSOPHY

What is the coach's philosophy concerning development? Does the strength and conditioning coach believe in no off days? Do they believe in high reps, low resistance? Do they believe in eccentric loading as a foundation for all exercises? Does the player development coach focus on volume or quality? Broad view or specificity? Where does the coach start with each player? What is the progression? Is it one size fits all? These are all important questions.

METHODOLOGY

Methodology is how coaches get players from Point A to Point Z. It involves the training aids, program design, frequency, intensity, etc. that will be used to take a player to their desired level and beyond. Methodology is, in my opinion, more about the track or path a player takes than the training aids and techniques that are being used. There is a finite set of skills needed to be considered highly proficient. Many different methods can be used to reinforce or teach a particular skill. However, the intent and focus needed to acquire the necessary skillsets remain the same.

RESULTS

Does your coach have a track record of improving athletes? Are the improvements substantial? Can these improvements be directly attributed to working with this particular coach?

What do others say about the coach's work and their players' improvements? Remember, every coach started somewhere. All coaches are on trial when they start out in this business. Even if the coach is new, how do they stack up in the other categories? What are their energy, presentation, and rapport with their clients like? This will tell you what you need to know to take a chance on a future star in their respective industry.

One last thing: if any coach that you speak with talks ill of other trainers and their training methods, steer clear. There are many good coaches out there. Because others don't do it in the same way as that coach, it doesn't mean they don't get results. No matter how much better one coach is than another coach, they should never belittle what others are doing.

REFLECT

How well have you selected trainers and coaches for your child? Have you chosen those who appeared to be knowledgeable at first, only to realize later that they didn't know what you thought they knew?

ACT

1. Find coaches in all three areas: player development, strength and conditioning, and mental toughness. Ask them the aforementioned questions. But don't act as though it's an interrogation. Many of these questions can be answered on the coach's website or social media pages. But a simple conversation with strategically placed questions will get you more information than you could ever have imagined.

2. If you have already started retaining coaches in these three specific areas to improve your young

athlete's performance, have you asked the questions mentioned above?

BONUS

<u>Key 8</u>

DO: Help Your Athlete Develop Ironclad Confidence

The most talked-about subject in the world of sports is confidence or mental toughness. But what is it really? As a parent, your goal is to know what it is and how to foster the development of that pivotal trait in your young athlete. Having studied under Dr. Jim Loehr, world-renowned sports psychologist, I learned that mental toughness is comprised of four key realms: physical, mental, emotional, and spiritual. If any one of these areas is off, then your "mental toughness"—confidence in adverse or difficult situations—will be affected.

If blood sugar is low (physical), it will be difficult for a player to have the steady hands needed to calmly knock down free throws to win the game. If a player has dozens of homework assignments due and is thinking about finishing their schoolwork immediately after the game, they could lose focus (mental) during a game, which could lead to costly turnovers. If a player has a heated argument with a loved one (emotional) and is feeling hurt or angry, their performance can be affected. Lastly, if a player's motivation for playing well is so that everyone will like them or to become the big person on campus, superior to others, then the spirit behind what the player is doing is off (spiritual).

Parents have a huge role in developing the type of confidence and mental toughness that is revealed in the research based PDI Smart™ Model by the Purpose Development Institute. Created by Master Purpose Development Coach Donald Jenkins and Dr. Lily Jenkins, it is the best system that I have seen in the space of developing the confidence of athletes. The Purpose Development Institute has become a world leader in helping parents make smarter decisions for parenting athletes. Their online Crushing Average parenting course is one of the top courses for equipping parents to make a quantum leap in helping athletes buy into a greater level of confidence and mental toughness. This course is instrumental in reducing the risk of projecting your own insecurities, fears, ego, biases, and traumas onto your child either verbally or energetically. It takes into consideration that we are energetic beings and that we can feel what people believe, no matter what they say.

Essentially, what I am saying is that the previous seven chapters are chapter 8! I have given you the template for building overall confidence and character in your young athlete. That is why I saved this "bonus" chapter for last. This book is my attempt to lead you to the ultimate goal of parenting: delivering a confident, high-character, well-rounded, and well-prepared person and player to the world!

Your job is a pivotal one. You are initially the training wheels on your child's bike. You will be the training wheels for a very long time. However, you, the training wheels, will eventually be taken off. You will still run alongside the bike for a little longer. Eventually, you will go into the house! That is how we should look at parenting—as stewards for guidance, not steerers to control. The more independent your child becomes, the greater their chance of adjusting to interdependency more easily, which is the highest level of interaction. It can only be on full display when one is truly confident in oneself.

Five-star recruit Courtney Ogden talks about how her dad tested her early as the "screaming parent" and then later transitioned into the wise guide of few words. Chris, her father, was a very good Division I basketball player at Murray State. Her mother, Carla, is a Spelman graduate and group strategy director. I have often said, in its totality, that they have displayed the "perfect" athletic parenting. Perfect isn't really perfect, hence the quotation marks.

Now, that doesn't mean we have agreed on every move. Not even close. We have had many spirited debates on this journey together as a team. We might argue about technique. However, we have rarely disagreed philosophically. They have navigated this journey by placing Courtney in positions that forced her to grow. Both have done very little coddling. Her father has allowed hard coaching and training. His selection of Courtney's team has been outstanding in my opinion. From choosing our company as the cornerstone of Courtney's player development to selecting FBC with Coach Mo as Courtney's travel team, he has been extremely intentional in his moves.

These moves have resulted in Courtney becoming extremely mature in how she handles particular situations like not playing well or team chemistry or being yelled at or coached hard. Very little fazes her. She has developed the ability to extract the message despite how the message is delivered. This is an emotional maturity that I lacked even as a college player. In addition, Chris has stepped in to fight Courtney's battles only when absolutely necessary. But Courtney normally handles her own business with a maturity that belies her age, having progressively developed these skills throughout the years.

Another incredible act of parenting is that of Che' Bledsoe whose daughter, Anriel Howard, I trained in high school. Anriel set many records at Texas A & M/Mississippi State and now competes in the WWE under the stage name Lash Legend. When Anriel started training with our company she was virtually unranked as the 2200th player at her position in the country. Within one year she had risen to be the 16th best player in the country at her position. The reason? Well, I could easily attribute her rise to our training. But I would only be sharing with you a small portion of the formula for Anriel's success. The biggest piece of the puzzle was Che's uncanny ability to make sound decisions with regards to putting Anriel in the right situations.

She also instilled this unwavering confidence in Anriel that, with the right resources and work ethic, she would be able to accomplish anything that she wanted to. Truly a masterful job.

We have many other examples of great athletic parenting, including Darroll Lawson, whose son, Josiah Lawson, is a high-level recruit. Darroll's focus on developing Josiah holistically shows in how Josiah plays and conducts himself. Sandra and Linzy Collins should also be commended. Their daughter, Diana Collins, another five-star recruit, has done an incredible job of navigating the pushing and pulling of parenting. There are many, many more of our parents who have absolutely done the best with what they have had to work with. Each should be lauded, applauded, and commended.

My Personal Road to Confidence

Before I give you the game plan for confidence, I would be remiss if I didn't share my own journey. I have to be totally honest and transparent about my journey. I pray that my incredible mom doesn't feel any type of way when she reads this. Her story is amazing. Her life has been amazing. She did the best that she could given what she had. Having had friction with my mom growing up, I could never, never understand why she was the way that she was. I was a true daddy's boy. One day my father and I were talking. He was my go-to. Any question about life, any question about anything, I asked him. And I asked him what it was like growing up poor. I will never forget his response. Never.

He pondered for second as he stared off into space. He said, "To be honest, Dorian, I don't think we were poor. We always had enough to eat. We always had clothes on our backs. And our lights and water were always on." Then he looked at me and said, "But your mom ..." He shook his head. "Now, son, they were poor!" So Daddy began to explain my mom's upbringing and the difficulties she faced. My mother is a direct descendent of the last slave ship to ever land in America: the Clotilda. Her grandfather, my great-grandfather, was one of the 110 who were on that ship.

Many books have been written about the community that was started by those who were dropped off—illegally, I might add—to fend for themselves in what is now known as Africatown, USA (Plateau, Alabama). Daddy began to explain to me how tough it was for my mom growing up. Her father died at age forty-four, leaving a wife and five kids, with my mom being the oldest. The result of that devastating loss was my grandmother, Henrietta Edwards Allen, literally having a breakdown. My mother, aged sixteen at the time, had to take charge of her three brothers and one sister while consoling and supporting my grandmother.

The stories were harrowing. They had to pile into one corner of the house with blankets to keep warm. They could see the ground through their floors because of the rotten wood. So much more that I dare not mention. But my mom did it! All while being the best female athlete and student at her school. It built a level of toughness in my mom that at times was unrelenting.

It also built great fear in her—a fear that was often passed on to us. Everything was doom, gloom, and even death. Because that was what her life had been like.

A great example of this was her approach to me learning to drive. Her words were that "cars kill people" as opposed to "cars are amazing inventions, but we have to respect them because they are heavy machines." This approach gave me an immense fear of driving. So much so that I failed my driving test three times! Make a mental note of that. It will be extremely important later.

In my athletic life, I was a prodigy—the fastest, strongest, highest-jumping little "freak" that you ever wanted to see. I started playing in second grade. I was so "trash" then that I can't even remember any of it. But by third grade, your boy (me) was "okay." I scored all but four of my team's points for the entire season. Won every game. I had two games where I had ten points. Doesn't sound impressive? Average score of a game was six to four. I led my third-grade team to the championship game. But we lost. I played terribly. My mom's reaction to other parents criticizing me during the game was that the way I played was embarrassing and that I should "apologize" to every single teammate. I remember feeling so embarrassed the next day when I got to school. I approached one of my teammates and started to cry. I told him that I apologized for being the reason we lost. Do you know what he said? He said, "For what? We don't win a single game if you don't play!" This was a nine-year-old who had greater wisdom and a more realistic perspective than some adults. It made me feel good. But the damage was done.

Also, because my mom couldn't handle the ridicule from the other parents in the stands (she felt it was in some way a reflection on her), I don't recall her ever staying for another game. The next game I remember her attending was during my senior year in high school. It had a lasting impact. My last game in high school? Four points. My last game in junior college? Four points. My last official game at University of North Florida? Four points. Last game at Spring Hill College? Four points. Craziest thing about this is that I was clutch. Two walk-off game winners in high school. Six walk-off game winners in college. Clutch free throws. Clutch blocks. Clutch steals. I was not afraid to take the shot and be the hero or goat—as in scapegoat. But it was something about rivalry games and championship games that brought me back, unconsciously, to that third-grade championship game. It took me years to make the connection.

Now, back to the driving test. Had I not failed three times, I more than likely wouldn't be writing this book. Those who know me know that I can roast! Where I live, they call it "joning." Where I am from, they call it "janking." Where I went to college (UNF), they called it "ranking." No matter what you call it, I was, and am, good at it. So, I was working at Checkers (a hamburger restaurant) prior to my senior year in high school, and one night we were roasting and my coworkers got wind of me flunking the driving part of the exam three times. They lit me up. Like, they were relentless. I held my own, but grenades were being thrown from every direction. Even though many of these geniuses had flunked the written part, they were still lighting me up! How do you flunk the shapes of signs and still laugh at me?

Well, my manager let a guy who had worked for him at another restaurant into the restaurant after hours. The guy heard the roasting, but he didn't think it was funny. He offered to teach me how to drive and guaranteed that I would pass on my next attempt. He just wanted me to help him with his hoop game. So I said, "That's a deal!" During the process, he noticed how negative I was about everything, using phrases like "I hope I have a good season" or "Maybe I will get a scholarship." I didn't always make eye contact. So he told me to "cut that shit out!"—his exact words.

His name was Terry Trotter, and without him, this story of my newfound confidence would never have happened. He changed my view of life. He took me to every gym in Mobile to play against the best and the toughest competition. He found basketball goals that seemed impossible—too high—to dunk in and would bet me that I couldn't dunk in those goals. I dunked in every one. He would also get on me when he thought I was getting too cocky with this newfound confidence.

By the way, I passed my driving test on the next try. This seemingly trivial accomplishment gave me a huge boost in confidence and the belief that I could conquer anything I set out to accomplish. The result? Becoming the second leading scorer in the city my senior year behind only High School All-American and Duke star Antonio Lang. Terry changed the words that I spoke to myself. He changed how I prepared. He was always throwing me into the fire—into some uncomfortable situation to see if I would sink or swim. I never sank.

Remember your words. They are powerful. I have spoken to the spirit of many athletes who seemed to be long shots. Yvonne Anderson, Adam Smith, Demetrius Davis, Denzail Jones, and DeQuan Jones are a few examples of those who simply needed someone who spoke life into them. I also added to their bag—a term used in basketball that denotes a sharpened and broadened skillset. As result, they have had tremendously fruitful careers. I believed in them. Each knew that I believed in them. I only spoke with certainty in my communication with them. Because of this, they have created some amazing stories. Our words can encourage or they can discourage. But when emotion is attached to those words, they become even more powerful. They can literally carry your child for a lifetime. Or those words can strangle the tree at the root. Be mindful of your power as a parent—or coach—to speak life.

So here is the road to ironclad confidence. Focus on the four aforementioned areas: physical, mental, emotional, and spiritual. Legitimate work on all of these should yield nothing but outstanding results.

Physical (Key/Chapter 7)

Make sure that your young player is prepared in every way possible in terms of the actual game of basketball. That means they are the most skilled that they can become. That they are the most conditioned that they can become. That they work on their IQ as much as they can. Make sure they understand schemes both offensively and defensively by watching footage with a qualified person. If no one is available, help them learn to watch footage correctly in order to gain the maximum benefit from it. The reason I've added watching footage and developing their basketball IQ is because these things can become the differentiator when it comes to maximizing their physical gifts.

Mental (Keys/Chapters 2, 3, 4, 5, and 6)

A high-performance athlete visualizes successful scenarios in their mind. But they accomplish it in two ways: first from a spectator standpoint, as if they were watching themselves play, and second through their own eyes, as if they were on the court face-to-face with their opponents. Research has shown that visualization can improve a person's golf scores and free-throw percentages without them ever touching the golf clubs or the basketball.

Emotional (Keys/Chapters 3, 4, 5, and 6)

Controlling emotions boils down to breathing. The technique of "box breathing" can greatly reduce anxiety during performance. Breathing techniques also allow the athlete to channel their frustration and shake off mistakes. Slower breathing reduces tension in the body and promotes keen awareness. Noticing when your child is tight and teaching them to focus solely on their breathing can reinforce the young athlete's ability to self-manage in high-stress situations.

Spiritual (Keys/Chapters 3, 4, 6, and 8)

This is the area that only the player can truly know. When I speak of spirit, I speak of the intent with which you do what you do. Oftentimes, I will say that the spirit behind what you are doing is all that matters. But again, only the player can determine why they are playing. Is it with pure intent? Is it for the love of the game or for the love of fame? What we chase often eludes us. When you cease the chase, what you want often comes to you—if you have what it is attracted to.

You have to be before you can be-come. Excellence is an everyday choice. You can't be mediocre and eventually become great. You have to be great in order to become great. Wanting to be your best isn't the same as wanting to be observed being the best! What others think of you will change with the wind. Focus on yourself. Focus on optimizing who you are.

However, I am no fool. When those cheers start coming, it can become an addiction. Just remember not to play for the applause. Just play so well that you get the applause. But only play for the applause of one person: yourself. You know when you have done your best, prepared your best, competed your best, and left it all on the floor.

Conclusion

So is that it? Yes, I am excited to say that it is indeed it! You are now more equipped to handle the rigors of raising a young athlete. Understanding your parenting style, accurately assessing everything about your child, allowing your child to grow from negative experiences, permitting your child to fight their own battles, teaching them how to eliminate excuses by limiting the excuses that you make for them, making sure your young player has the type of game that coaches love, and finally helping develop the type of confidence that almost ensures their success in any endeavor—you now have all those tools in your belt.

Whew! That seems like a lot! But in reality, it isn't. I need you to approach it like I approached writing this book: one page at a time. This is, in most cases, a long short-term process. This development takes place over years. You can compare it to investing early vs. investing late. The type of money needed to yield the same return, had you been investing all along, is astronomical in comparison to the small amounts that were required when you started early in your career or early in your children's college funds. Growth in player development is strikingly similar to financial growth. It is not linear. It is exponential. If you understand this, you understand the power that you actually possess to help your young athlete reach their dreams!

Lastly, this book is not to be read once and discarded. It should be referenced often. The REFLECT and ACT sections after each chapter should be revisited and reevaluated as your young athlete continues to grow. Nothing is permanent. Things can often change. Each season, each new team, and each new endeavor poses an opportunity to see if you are still adhering to the principles outlined in this book. Assess thoroughly and often. More importantly, look ahead. Anticipate where things are going. Watch for trends that could derail your child's success—for example, noticing that a once hard-working kid is becoming complacent. Continue to be the guide your child needs.

It is my sincere hope that this book will bless you on this rewarding journey!

Made in the USA
Middletown, DE
27 September 2023